Let's Remember....

when TEXAS
WAS A
REPUBLIC

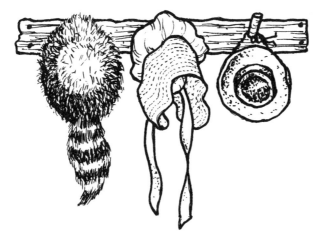

Written and Illustrated by Betsy Warren

1983 • HENDRICK-LONG PUBLISHING COMPANY • DALLAS

CONTENTS

ISBN 0-937460-09-5

1983 copyright © by Hendrick-Long, Dallas, Texas

A NEW COUNTRY—1836

Texas was owned by Spain for 302 years. Then it was ruled by Mexico for 15 years. In 1836, Texans fought Santa Anna and the Mexican army at the Battle of San Jacinto. General Sam Houston led the Texas soldiers to victory. Texas was freed from Mexican rule. Santa Anna went back to Mexico and promised never to fight again.

The people of Texas elected Sam Houston to be the first president of their new country. It was called the *Republic of Texas*.

President Houston asked Stephen F. Austin and other Texas leaders to help him govern the new Republic according to a Constitution which had been written. The Constitution was a set of rules to guide the people in making a strong government. It said that people of Texas would elect senators and representatives to meet together and make laws for the Republic. A Supreme Court of 3 to 8 men would be the final judge of these laws.

Stephen F. Austin

Mirabeau Lamar

George Childress

4 Henry Smith

Thomas Rusk

J. Pinckney Henderson

The FIRST CAPITAL—1836

Columbia was the first capital of the Republic of Texas. It was a small town near the mouth of the Brazos River. For four months, 14 senators and 29 representatives held meetings in Columbia.

In January of 1837, the capital was moved to the new town of Houston. Most of the people lived in tents or log cabins in Houston. Streets were often filled with mud because it rained so often. President Houston's house was a two-room log cabin. The capitol was an unfinished building with a leaky roof.

TEXAS RANGERS

Sam Houston and the lawmakers were often discouraged about the problems in starting a new country. The war with Mexico had ruined farms and towns. No one could raise money to build new shops or farms. Soldiers were needed to protect the settlers from outlaws, thieves, and Indians, but there was no money to pay them. Only a few Texas Rangers could be hired to ride over the land to try to keep law and order.

TROUBLES with the INDIANS

Indians were angry with white settlers who came into their areas. They often attacked farmers as they worked in their fields. At night, they stole horses and burned crops.

In 1836, Comanche Indians raided Fort Parker. They carried off a little girl—Cynthia Ann Parker, and her brother. Cynthia Ann grew up as an Indian and became the wife of a chief. Later, one of their sons, Quanah Parker, was the last great chief of the Comanche nation.

During many battles, both the Texans and the Indians suffered great losses. Some of the Indian tribes left the country to live in Mexico.

A NEW PRESIDENT—1838

After two years, the Texans elected Mirabeau Lamar to be president of the Republic. President Lamar chose a new capital. It was the tiny settlement of Waterloo on the Colorado River. Its name was changed to AUSTIN in honor of Stephen F. Austin. The lawmakers met in a small frame building to work out the problems of the Republic.

Before long, Texas leaders were able to borrow money from the United States to pay debts left from the war with Mexico. They also lent some of the money to the settlers so they could build homes, farms, and shops. They passed laws which gave land for public schools and for the new settlers who came to Texas.

8

DIPLOMAT from FRANCE—1840

France and England were the first European countries to accept Texas as a new country. The French sent a diplomat, Alphonse de Saligny, to the Republic, hoping he would work out ways for France to trade goods with Texas.

Saligny built a fine house, kitchen, and stables on a hill near the Austin capitol. His house still stands today as the oldest in Austin.

ANOTHER CAPITAL—1841

In 1841, Texans voted to make Sam Houston president for the second time. He took the capital back to the town of Houston. A few weeks later, it was moved to Washington-on-the-Brazos where the lawmakers met upstairs over a store. The capital stayed there for three years.

President Houston and his helpers worked to find ways for Texans to sell their cotton, rice, lumber, and other products to foreign countries. When markets were found, the settlers gradually began to be more prosperous.

MEXICO INVADES TEXAS

In 1842, Santa Anna, the Mexican president, once again sent soldiers to try to capture Texas. He had broken his promise not to fight anymore.

The Mexican army captured San Antonio, Goliad, and Refugio. Then the soldiers returned to Mexico. A short while later, they came back to take San Antonio again. When 750 Texas soldiers gathered to drive out Santa Anna's army, the Mexicans hurried back across the Rio Grande. They never came back to fight in Texas again.

SETTLERS *from* EUROPE

During the 1840s, thousands of people from foreign countries settled in Texas. They came by ship from Austria, Poland, France, Ireland, Germany, and other countries of Europe.

Although most of the settlers were farmers, some were teachers, lawyers, and doctors. Others were blacksmiths, wagon makers, leather tanners, and woodworkers. They all helped make Texas a better place to live.

HENRI CASTRO—1843

In 1843, Henri Castro brought 400 people from France and Germany to make farms in the wilderness near San Antonio. They suffered from sickness, lack of food, poor crops, and Indian attacks. Even so, they built sturdy homes and good farms. By 1846 there were 2000 people settled around the town of Castroville.

Henri Castro

Solms-Braunfels

SOLMS-BRAUNFELS—1845

Many people left Germany to become pioneers in Central Texas. The first large group was led by Prince Solms-Braunfels. In 1845, he and his colonists started the town of New Braunfels on the Comal River. They established farms, shops, schools, churches, and singing societies.

Other towns started by the Germans during the Republic were: LaGrange (1837), Industry (1838), Cat Spring (1844), Brenham (1844), and New Ulm (1845).

EVERYDAY LIFE in the REPUBLIC

HOUSES

Early settlers built log cabins for their homes, barns, and shops. A small cabin could be built in two days by five or six men.

When sawmills were started, logs could easily be cut into boards. Soon, large frame houses of pine, oak, and cedar took the place of log cabins. Settlers also learned to use native stone, adobe, and brick for their buildings.

FOOD

Each farm had cattle, pigs, and sometimes a milk cow. All of the settlers grew corn, sweet potatoes, and sugarcane. They gathered wild plants for food and medicines.

The men hunted deer, turkey, buffalo, and wild geese for food. Fish were plentiful in rivers and streams. Fruit and nut trees grew wild in the countryside. Honey taken from bee-trees was a special treat.

CLOTHING

Farmers planted cotton and raised sheep to supply cotton and wool. Women wove threads of cotton and wool into cloth and made "homespun" clothes for the entire family. To add colors, they mixed dyes from berries, treebark, nuts, and other plants. Shoes and moccasins were cut and sewn from deer and buffalo hides. Stockings, caps, and gloves were knitted by women and girls in the family. They also made soap and candles from ashes and animal fats.

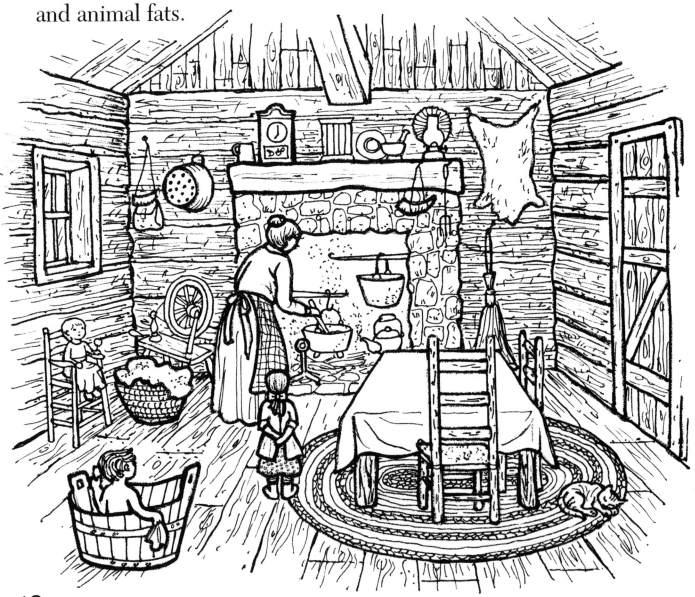

SCHOOLS

Settlers wanted schools for their children. They built one-room log cabins and hired someone to teach for several months during the year. Since few families had money, the teacher was usually paid with a cow and chickens or a piece of land.

Most students stayed in school only long enough to learn to read and do simple arithmetic. They were needed at home to work on the farms and plantations.

The first college started during the Republic was at Rutersville, a small settlement near LaGrange. It was founded in 1840 with 63 students. Baylor University, chartered in 1845, is the oldest college remaining from Republic days.

CHURCHES

Church meetings were held in a school house or in a home. Ministers and priests traveled on horseback or by wagon between settlements to perform marriages and hold other services. In summer months, wagonloads of people sometimes gathered at a campground. Sitting under brush arbors, they sang hymns, visited, and listened to the preaching for several days before returning home.

When towns became larger and more prosperous, the people built permanent schools and churches.

AMUSEMENTS

Although settlers worked hard from sunrise to sunset, they had time for fun, too. Footracing and horseracing were favorite pastimes for the men and boys. Women gathered in homes for "Quilting Bees" where they sewed and stitched quilts for each other.

Families met to make music, read poetry, essays, and conundrums, and to perform plays. Young people often rode horseback for many miles to attend dances and parties called "taffy pulls".

John James Audubon

Ferdinand Lindheimer

Charles Wright

NATURALISTS

Naturalists wanted to study unknown plants, animals, and land formations in Texas.

JOHN JAMES AUDUBON came from the United States in 1837 to study birds along the coast. He and his sons made fine paintings of Texas birds and animals.

CHARLES WRIGHT, also from the United States, came the same year. During the next 13 years, he walked thousands of miles to find samples of plants and insects to send to schools and museums. Books and articles were written about his discoveries.

In 1845, FERDINAND LINDHEIMER, a German, settled in New Braunfels. In the hills of Central Texas he collected samples of wildflowers and sent them to scientists and museums in the United States and Europe. His name was given to more than 30 wildflowers and he became known as the "Father of Texas Botany"

ARTISTS and WRITERS

Painters and writers helped the rest of the world learn about the Texas Republic.

MARY AUSTIN HOLLEY is remembered for her letters and diaries describing Texas. She also wrote "History of Texas", a book which was widely read in the United States.

THEODORE GENTILZ of France came to live in Castroville in 1844. His paintings of Indians and scenes around San Antonio show how people lived at that time. He also taught art for 30 years at St. Mary's Hall, a college in San Antonio.

CARL VON IWONSKI came from Germany to New Braunfels in 1845. He became well-known as an artist who painted portraits of German pioneers and scenes of Central Texas.

Mary Austin Holley

Carl von Iwonski

Theodore Gentilz

NEWSPAPERS

The only way for people to have news of other places was by talking with travelers or reading newspapers and letters. In 1836 there was only one newspaper, the TELEGRAPH and TEXAS REGISTER. By 1840, there were 13 newspapers in Texas. Many of these were published in Austin and came out more than once a week. Since few people lived west of the Colorado River, there were no newspapers in that area.

The GALVESTON NEWS, founded in 1842, is the oldest surviving newspaper.

TRANSPORTATION

ROADS

During the days of the Republic, it took a long time to get from one place to another. People walked great distances. Others traveled by horseback or in wagons drawn by oxen, mules, or horses.

Roads were dusty trails which turned into muddy bogs when it rained. Since there were few bridges, ferry boats carried people and wagons across the rivers while horses and cattle swam.

The oldest road was called "El Camino Real—The King's Highway". Its dirt tracks stretched from the Rio Grande to Nacogdoches. Other roads, called "traces", were like narrow paths which had been cut through the wilderness.

STAGECOACHES and INNS

Between the towns, pack mules and ox-drawn covered wagons carried freight goods. Stage coaches took passengers and mail from town to town over the bumpy roads.

One of the first hotels where travelers could stop to rest was Fanthorp Inn. It was built in 1834 in East Texas at present-day Anderson. It was the best known inn during the Republic and is still standing today.

BOATS

Since rivers were too shallow to be used by steamboats, large rafts and flatbottom boats carried cotton bales, pecans, hides, and other goods down the rivers to coastal ports. These products were then taken by ship across the Gulf to New Orleans to be loaded onto ships going to foreign countries throughout the world. Returning ships brought back goods to be sold in Texas.

Keelboats, propelled by sails and poles, were also used on the Texas rivers for carrying freight and people.

INDUSTRIES

FISHING, LUMBER MILLS

Along the coast, men made a living by fishing in the Gulf. They sold their catches of shrimp, oysters, and deep-sea fish in the nearby towns. Houston, Indianola, and Velasco were important fishing ports during the Republic.

Wood was needed for necessities such as houses, furniture, boats, and wagons. Most of it came from the huge forests of pine, cedar, and cypress trees in East Texas. After being cut, the logs were floated down the Neches and Sabine Rivers to the mills which sawed them into lumber. The first steam sawmill had been built by 1830 near Houston. From it, lumber was hauled by wagons or by boat into all parts of Central Texas.

TEXAS BECOMES A STATE

During the days of the Republic, many small settlements grew into bustling towns. Farms and plantations were large and prosperous. However, most Texans believed that the Republic was not strong enough to be a country by itself. They were afraid that Mexico would conquer them. So they voted to send representatives to Washington, D.C. to ask if Texas could be a part of the United States.

At first, people in the United States did not want Texas because it had slaves. However, they did not want Texas to belong to any other country. Finally, in 1845, the United States agreed that Texas could join them as the 28th state.

A NEW FLAG—1846

In Austin, Anson Jones had been elected as president of the Republic. He announced to the people of Texas that they would be citizens of the United States. On February 16, 1846, President Jones took down the flag of the Republic. A crowd had gathered to watch. As he raised the flag of the United States, President Jones said "The Republic of Texas is no more."

This is how Texas became a part of the United States.

CAN YOU REMEMBER?

1. Who was the first president of the Republic of Texas?_____

2. Where was the first capital?_____

3. Why were Texas Rangers needed?_____

4. Who captured Cynthia Ann Parker?_____

5. What was the new name given to the town of Waterloo?____

6. Name 3 European countries from which settlers came._____

_____

7. How did people travel in the Republic?_____

8. What did Ferdinand Lindheimer do?_____

9. Where did children go to school?_____

10. Why did Texas want to be a part of the United States?_____

_____

WHAT CAME FIRST?

Use the numbers 1,2,3,4,5 to show which event happened first.

_____ the flag of the United States was raised over Texas.

_____ Sam Houston was elected as the first president of the Republic.

_____ Texans fought the Mexican army at the Battle of San Jacinto.

_____ The city of Austin became the capital of the Republic.

_____ Henri Castro brought settlers to establish the colony of Castroville.

IS IT TRUE?

Write a T before each sentence which is true.

_____ Santa Anna was president of the Republic of Texas.

_____ The town of Austin was the first capital.

_____ France sent a diplomat to the Republic of Texas.

_____ Henri Castro brought settlers to Dallas.

_____ Settlers built houses of cement.

_____ El Camino Real was a river.

_____ Sam Houston was president of the Republic two times.

_____ Texas Rangers helped protect the early settlers.

MAKE THEM MATCH

Draw a line from the word to the picture that matches it.

Texas flag

Austin capitol

Texas Ranger

cotton

deer

ox

wildflower

keelboat

stagecoach

turkey

JOIN THE DOTS

. . . and see the animal that pulled wagons and plows for the early Texas settlers.

CROSSWORD PUZZLE

ACROSS
1. Texas was a _____
2. Something knitted by women
3. A log cabin was built for a _____

DOWN
1. Animal hunted by settlers
2. Food
3. Senators and Representatives made _____
4. Columbia was the first _____

WORDS YOU WILL NEED
Republic
buffalo
laws
rice
school
caps
capital

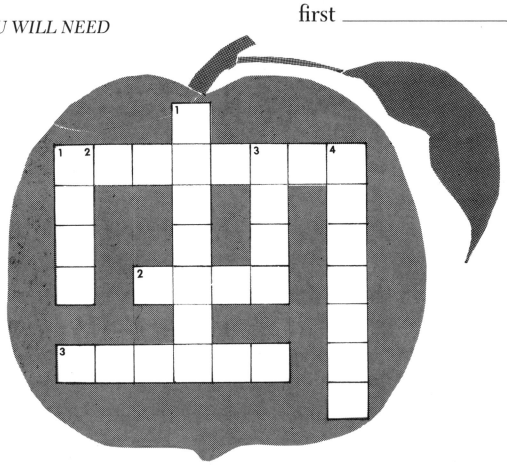